CREATIVE

WRITING

- FROM THINK TO INK

LEARN HOW TO UNLEASH YOUR CREATIVE SELF AND
DISCOVER WHY YOU DON'T NEED 1000 WRITING
PROMPTS TO BLAST AWAY YOUR WRITER'S BLOCK AND
IMPROVE YOUR WRITING SKILLS

Table Of Contents

Introduction: What is Creativity Anyway, and Why Create at all?

When you were a tiny baby, your head was full of mostly nothing and the world was new and unknown. You barely had the skill to move yourself around the environment, and you most definitely lacked the skill to do what humans are most know for – communication.

As you grew and developed, though, something strange started to happen. The people around you, the things in your world - you began to understand that they could be *reached*. That in your infant isolation there was still a way to reach out and touch someone else's experience. You saw all around you evidence of this magical skill that you had yet to develop: language.

Almost every infant learns to talk, and many believe that impulse comes from this original yearning to reach out and connect, to speak and be heard, to breach the abyss between one and the other.

At the root of all creative expression is a deep, inborn and very human desire to be heard.

Since before we were old enough to understand it, we've tried to master this almost god-like ability to shape symbols and concepts, reach into the mind of someone else and affect their hearts and minds, to bring about changes in the world, to connect and understand and share with another human being.

I believe that it's at this early stage that writers are born. Children gradually learn that some words are more correct than others, that some have greater effect, that some words get you into trouble and some words bring you closer to what you want. And when you eventually developed a sense of identity, you realized that words are the special tool that allows you to speak your mind, to make your desires known.

Language is a window into the soul.

For the writers among us, the urge to communicate more clearly, more beautifully, and in new ways never really left us. With the right words, new worlds can be created, new ideas can be incubated and grown, great heights and depths can be reached. Every brilliant idea had its first home in the written or spoken word, and if you are a writer or aspire to be one, you most likely understand this power better than anything.

So, why write?

Why be creative at all?

Creativity is perhaps the most uniquely human characteristic, and it's no exaggeration that many have linked it to the divine. Creativity is the ability to look out over the vista of reality, and have the courage to wonder, "what if this was some other way?"

All change and growth begins with the creativity of imagining something different. In this book, we'll be talking about writing specifically, but creativity isn't fussy, and it's quite likely that opening the door on your innate creativity will invite all sorts of new skills and insights into your life, not just the verbal ones.

Let's start at the very beginning.

Our creativity journey will begin in infancy, and we'll go back to that wondering child who made the first momentous leap with his first word.

Today's exercise is broad and simple, but ponder it long enough and you'll start to uncover new, unexpected aspects. Ask yourself this simple question: *why write at all?*

Take a moment or two to answer this for yourself, but don't be satisfied with a superficial answer. It's great if your answer is, "to share my message," but take it further – what does that really *mean*? Why bother sharing your message? What's so special about that message anyway?

Once you've condensed down some of these sentiments, you'll have found something that will be incredibly valuable to your writing career, wherever it takes you: your purpose. Tapping into the deep roots of *why* you are compelled to write at all is a brilliant way to unlock your true motivations and your ultimate reason for that urge to take what's in your head and put it out there in the world.

How to find that "Big Why"

- What is the response to your writing you hope to receive, if any?

- How will you feel if nobody ever reads your work or understands what you're trying to get across?

- What, in essence, is your message?

- In the most general sense, do you feel heard in the world? Who do you have something to say to? Why? If you had the attention of the entire world for five whole minutes, what would you want to say to everybody?

- Picture people reading the best possible work you could hope to produce in this lifetime. Now, think carefully, what is their ideal reaction? In what ways do you want to move them? How will you know you've been successful?

Bear with me a little while I dwell on the fluffy stuff. Plenty of writing advice out there is focused on the nuts and bolts of writing – how to do it, when, how to market it and where, etc. But this is not that sort of book. If you want to learn to write more compellingly, with more skill and expertise, you can do it, easily. The really tricky bit, though, is understanding *why*.

Uncover this *why* for yourself and you get in touch with the inexhaustible engine of your creativity. The human core of why we bother to create at all. Get to know this root well and you will not need gimmicky books full of writing prompts to blast away your writer's block. You will not need "inspiration" or 31 awesome tips and tricks. When you were a baby, *something* made you open your mouth and speak. Understand the thing that inspired you to do this, and you're more than half way to being the creative, productive and generative human being you were destined to be.

Chapter 1: Desire – the Root of Creativity

If nothing momentous emerged for you with previous exercise, don't sweat it. You might have had a breakthrough and realized that deep down, your drive to create and express comes from a long buried need for affirmation that started in your childhood ...or, you may merely feel that life is hard and you just like writing goofy things that make people laugh.

It doesn't matter. Even if an answer isn't forthcoming, keep asking it in the background. The answer may already be stirring somewhere inside you, waiting to come out soon. Let it be.

In this chapter, we move on to a more specific examination of how we can connect more authentically to that gorgeous, white hot, fantastic, almost genius kind of expression we all long for.

Have you had any moments like this?

Moments where you created something you were intensely proud of, almost gobsmacked by the joy and thrill of it being yours, and being *good*. We have all known creative competence before, and we've all known the satisfaction of making something exist that didn't exist before. It's almost an addictive feeling, isn't it?

We've briefly looked at the origin of creativity in the previous exercise. Wanting to be heard, in the most general sense, is at the core of many people's desire to write a play, paint a picture, go on stage or type out the first chapter of a sweeping sci-fi fantasy novel.

If you're feeling a little dry, or a little uninspired, there's one sure fire way to juice up your creative machine again: desire.

To reach out into the world takes a stirring, a yearning, a wanting.

What do you want?

This chapter's exercise is going to be a flight of fancy, and I'm giving you permission right now to run with it, as far as you like.

With a notebook, start jotting down ideas and impressions around the central title – *what do you want?* Don't think about it too deeply, don't dawdle and imagine someone else reading your work to see if you're "doing it right" ...just ask the deepest stirrings in your heart and mind what they crave, and put it on the paper.

Do you have a hunger for more love and beauty in your life? Do you wish things made more sense? Are you lonely? Bored and desperate for something exciting to happen in life? Do you feel broke a lot of the time and feel a secret desire for ease and luxury? Do you wish your life were quirkier and more special? Do you wish you were popular? Do you crave a sense of purpose or prestige or the stability of a stable job? More money? Do you long for harmony and work that really fulfills you? Adventure? Do you want a little romance in your life? The thrill of some danger? More intellectual stimulation? Do you really really wish you could just buy an X Box already?

Go wild. Don't put any limits on yourself.

When you switch on this sense of desire and grasping in yourself, you reacquaint with the first little seeds of creativity. Necessity, as they say, is the mother of invention. Many beautiful things exist in this world solely because their creators were sick of living in a world where it didn't exist.

Have you ever had the feeling that you could do something better than how you see it being done around you? Explore that. Do you ever look at someone's life and feel a yearning to be more like them? Write it down. What is the flavor and tone of your big dreams – the stuff you'd do in a fantasy life? Look at all the things you hate about the world around you right now. After all, what do authors do, fundamentally, except argue with reality?

Writing and putting out your own unique message takes a few special elements, and the first is the desire that things *should be different somehow*. This starts with desire. Today, tap into that – this yearning and stirring is a powerful source of energy that will get you through many difficult nights of self doubt, or through many boring mornings when you feel like you lack the enthusiasm to get started.

Perhaps you're a technical writer who has a strong desire for clarity and elegance in life. Maybe you find the world utterly boring and colourless and get a thrill out of creating an alternate universe where enthralling characters battle out their bizarre story in crystal palaces in faraway galaxies. Maybe you're just damn opinionated and you're ready to give people a piece of your mind.

Whatever it is, take a moment to get cosy with your desire. Of course, this isn't a self help book and we all know that wanting something doesn't mean getting it, but knowing where to go to find your juiciest, most abundant source of creative energy is a powerful tool for any creative. Own it.

Chapter 2: Having the Guts to Say Something

So, we've had a brief look at our Big Why and started putting out feelers to find those delicious roots of desire that inform all our creative impulses. Now, ladies and gentlemen, allow me to introduce you to the Closet Writer (although I believe you're already quite well acquainted with this character...)

The Closet Writer works some job or other, which he likes some amount but not overly so, and he has colleagues who would be shocked to learn that he writes in his spare time. The Closet Writer (let's call him Ned, shall we? In my story, I'm going to give him dark eyes and suspiciously smooth hands and a mole on his cheek with three hairs in it ...this is my story after all and that's the way I'm going to make it.)

Ned has scores of notebooks at home, all filled with the beginnings of novels, with grand plans and outlines of stories, with character sketches and bold ideas. He has poems he wrote in university that he was proud of but now hides in back pages of journals, letting them slowly go yellow. He occasionally shares these things with his mother and sometimes his girlfriend, and they like it, but then nothing happens and he goes back to scribbling behind closed doors, with vague notions of sharing his work "someday".

Deep down, Ned has one belief that keeps his scribblings hidden and almost shameful: that he doesn't have the right to speak. That artists are some sort of special species who are bright and brilliant and that he's not really one of them. So he calls himself an "*aspiring* writer" and blushes and changes the topic when people ask him about it at parties. He likes to think of himself as massively talented, but misunderstood. He doesn't take criticism well and one day, when he sees a less talented and completely ordinary friend succeed at writing something and publishing it, he gets bitter and writes off his success, "Well it's easy to get trash like that published, obviously. It's harder to find a market for stuff that's written properly, it's the sorry state of publishing today."

Any of this sounding familiar? Unlike other minority groups and closet-dwellers, however, life does not get better for Ned. He goes to the grave, as Thoreau said, "with his song still in him." Ned had the tiny flickers of desire and creativity and yearning in him, lacked the guts to put it out there, and that's that.

Millions of epic sagas, brilliant songs, beautiful poems and movies that might have been blockbusters have died along with these people who didn't believe they had the right to ask the world to pay attention. Being creative takes a certain amount of audacity, and the sorry truth is that most of us are just too afraid to speak up and say our bit.

We're taught from childhood that all our efforts will be judged and ranked along with the efforts of our peers. We're raised in school and work environments that discourage boasting and unique expression. We value conformity and like only those ideas that are financially profitable. We penalize difference and diversity in others, all the while stifling it in ourselves and trying to win approval rather than understanding our unique selves and having the guts to broadcast them.

So Ned says, "Oh nothing, don't worry, I have nothing to say" and the world doesn't argue with him, and he goes on scratching notes privately, and that, ladies and gentlemen, is a tragedy that rivals Shakespeare's.

Today, look at your desires and your Big Why. Try to see if you carry any shame or embarrassment about it. I'm not just talking about being sheepish about exploring your gift for writing absolutely filthy erotica or a hush-hush hobby where you write terribly nerdy fan fiction.

Ask yourself honestly if you censor your message in the belief that you don't deserve to have one. I can tell you one thing right now: famous authors, well-known speakers and all the rest – they weren't any more or less special than you. They didn't come into this world with their fame already in tact. They had something to say, and they took the leap of faith and said it. In fact, some authors were only really appreciated after they died. But they understood that keeping quiet when they had something to share was far worse than enduring the fear of just saying it.

- Are you secretly sabotaging yourself because you're "not a real writer"?

- Do you call yourself an "aspiring writer" or call your craft a hobby or a dream or speak about it in ways that undermine your seriousness? "Author" and "authority" share the same root – and for good reason. Do you have a sense of *authority*, literally?

- Are you generally unconfident in life? Do you hold your tongue or act like a martyr in your relationships? Do you sell yourself short?

- Do you care too much what other people think about you?

Chapter 3: Finding Your Own Style and Voice

It's easy to recognize a young writer – they sound like someone else. Find a fledgling author, look at the books they're busy reading at the moment and I can guarantee you their work will reflect that. This is not necessarily a bad thing, though.

Little children learn to speak from their parents, but eventually, they use that same language to express their *own* ideas. Writing is the same. It can be tricky to create something that is 100% unique and fresh, but again, this is not a problem. There are billions of people in the world, and only so many ways to say a thing, and frankly, all art is somewhere along the line "inspired" from other art.

Finding your own unique voice and style is not something that can be rushed. It's something that you grow into slowly, with practice. In the meantime, use other authors for inspiration and direction. Many people do this the wrong way round: they realize they don't have their own unique writing style, and so try to create one by deliberately tinkering with style elements until they can say, "there, that looks unique enough, I've never seen that before, I can claim this as my own now."

Often, though, "unique" is just shorthand for "authentic". An effective piece of writing is not merely a gimmick put together from a novel use of grammar and style. It's a complex blend of content, style and intention. It all goes back, in other words, to the Big Why.

A slower (but more solid) way to unearth your own personal style is just to remove anything that's getting in the way of your own natural expression. Tap into your real motivations for writing, get to the root of your message, and then write – your style will emerge on its own, if you let it.

In this chapter, we'll look at a constructive way to start including elements from writers you admire without simply aping them and losing your own unique voice.

First, start out by identifying two or three writers that you admire. Pick someone you've read a lot or even better, someone who has a very *distinctive* style.

Ask yourself, what is it about this writing that appeals to you? Go into as much details as possible. For example, you could say something like, "this author uses technically simple language and very tight, concise sentences but somehow manages to talk about very big, abstract topics. He leaves a lot to the reader's imagination. It's informal writing, almost stream of consciousness. It's got a bit of a nasty edge to it, like it comes from someone's hidden, unspoken mind. It looks like it's always in first person. It's usually about topics like relationships and family. Whenever I read this author, I feel very sad and wistful, and the stories often have a bit of bitterness in them somehow, which I like..."

Now that you've identified some elements in the style (notice how I've included not just grammar but also tone, mood, content etc.), ask yourself if there's anything in your writing that mirrors that. Look for similarities. For example, you may notice that both you and your favourite author like to dwell on the complexities of relationships, and that both have a bit of a sad tone to them. But you may also notice that where that author is curt and minimalist, you prefer writing longer, more descriptive sentences.

Do this with the other authors you've chosen.

The key here is to find out ways that other authors have already achieved something you're trying to do yourself. Look at things that resonate and then look at the cold mechanics of the thing – when your author succeeds at writing in a way you'd like, ask exactly how they did it. Feel free to incorporate *those* elements into your writing.

You could also do this by asking yourself about the ways you are different from a particular author, and amplifying that. Do you know any authors who have a similar message to you but a completely different way of expressing their thoughts? Do you read a blogger who shares your style of writing but about completely different subjects?

Merely imitating other artists and writers is not as smart as looking carefully at why and how other creative people are doing their work, and what you can learn from them. Sometimes, getting your own voice is merely a question of reading something and thinking, "Man, I could do this better!"

Chapter 4: Being a Writer 24/7

Writers write even when they're not writing.

When I was young, in fact, most of my "writing" involved walking around and looking at grass. By the time I turned up at the blank page, I already had fully formed ideas and my writing was merely the act of putting things down so I wouldn't forget them.

Writing is not just the physical act of typing on a laptop or scribbling in a notebook. Writing encompasses everything it takes to bring you to that moment where you're crafting the literal words – and that includes more or less your entire existence!

Everything you've experienced in your life, the dreams you have at night, your breakfast, the thoughts that bubble up as you commute to work – all of these things go directly or indirectly into your creation.

So, for this chapter, abandon the notion that writing is something you sit down to do for an hour or two and then forget about the rest of the time while you do the rest of your life. Writers are always switched on. Who knows when the next idea will come to fruition? Who knows what things you'll think of, or when a particularly awesome turn of phrase will spring to mind?

Give your brain something to work on and it will do it even when you sleep, or when you zone out and wash the dishes. Here are some daily exercises you can start doing to slip into your role as a 24/7, full time and always-on writer:

- Play with words, everywhere, all day, every day. Look at shop signs. When a person passes you in the street, quickly think of a metaphor that describes their eyes. Think of puns and jokes throughout the day. Use new words you pick up and listen carefully to the sounds of them in songs, or the rhythm and rhyme of particular words. Write down things that stand out for you.

- Keep a collection of quotes you like, copy out sentences that came out of articles and almost slapped you in the face they were so striking. Highlight bits in books you liked. Keep a dream journal for poignant and strange images to inspire you. Become curious about images, ideas, sounds and words around you ...and collect the ones that speak to you.

- If you're writing dialogue, listen to real life dialogue and get a feel for the natural flow of it. If you're writing a description of a place, go to places like it and immerse yourself there. If you're exploring a character, make it a blend of people you actually know.

- Carry a notebook around with you at all times, or else a voice recorder if you're feeling fancy. Your smartphone will do in a pinch. Many brilliant things have happened to authors while they're getting their pedicures or waiting in line at the post office – have a notebook to catch those little sparks of inspiration when they happen. Who knows what you can do with them later...

- Don't be like Ned and keep your writing stashed away all in secret. Buy organizers, files and folders – whatever you need to keep what comes out of your head safe and cherished.

- Open up. Inspiration is out there, floating, like some sort of radiation. Be receptive to it. This means making your sensory channels extra sensitive to all the fantastic things that are unfolding around you all day long. Really *look* at things. Listen to new music. Eat new foods. Touch things.

Chapter 5: Pride, Ego and Growth

Writing is an inherently narcissistic activity. You know those people who glibly mumble that they don't care about what anyone thinks because they only write for themselves and blah blah blah? Yeah, don't listen to them. We all write for a reason, and writing means nothing without an audience. Even if you never show your work to another living soul, well, you still wrote it *for* someone. That's the way that language works.

That someone may have only been in your head somewhere, and you may have been writing to them all along, unbeknownst to you. You might be writing to an imagined reader in the future, to a version of yourself, to your deceased mother, to a rival. But unless it's a grocery list, I can guarantee that every scrap of writing was written for a reason, and *for someone.*

This is a good thing. A crucial feature of any communication is that it starts at point A, and travels to *point B* – even if you're not entirely sure who's at point B just yet.

Now, as long as this is the case, you as an author are opening yourself up to a bit of a nasty reality: the possibility of a poor reception. The fact is, there is always the risk of miscommunication and misunderstanding. The possibility that even if you're understood, you can still be rejected. People who claim to not care about this are, I believe, in denial because the fact is so hard to digest.

Many people have never recovered from the first pain of having shared and expressed themselves only to find that their audience was unmoved, uninterested or worse, actively scornful. Putting out a creative effort is like baring your soul, and to have someone sneer at it can be a feeling almost worse than death.

It's no wonder that being creative and sharing your work with others is a project so fraught with ego. When someone rejects what you've slaved and laboured to create, it's easy to shut down and think they're wrong, that they're being hostile. It's easy to launch into believing that their opinion was worthless to you anyway, that they merely didn't understand you, that their taste in art was crappy all along, that you in turn judge them, that they're jealous, that they don't know what they're talking about, and on and on and on...

Now, while this reaction to criticism is entirely understandable, it doesn't mean it's something you should accept.

Luckily for writers, fantastic opportunities for growth and self-development exist. Unluckily, they exist in a difficult-to-access location on the other side of rejection and criticism. This growth is only available to those writers who have the guts to acknowledge that they could improve, and should. It's a kind of growth that only comes *after* the bravery of facing up to weaknesses and doing the difficult work of being better.

The tricky thing about big, fat, stupid egos is that nobody will ever really admit to having one! Read the following sentences and see if you've honestly ever felt them or expressed them. Tick all that apply:

- When someone doesn't like my work, I secretly think they just don't "get" it

- My writing is only for a small group of people anyway, and I'm not writing for those people who don't like me

- I'm only writing for myself, I don't care what anyone thinks

- I would join a writing group, but I'd prefer *professional* advice, not just the uninformed opinions of strangers

- Non-writers don't understand the struggle anyway, so their opinion means nothing to me

- I've done my best to express myself, if people don't understand, it's on them to try to interpret my work, not on me to explain it better

- If people don't like my work, I might as well just stop writing

- I believe people are generally vicious and cruel to writers, and I'm not willing to open myself up to that

- Unless I can be guaranteed a good reception, I don't want to risk sharing my work

- I would rather die than share an imperfect work in progress

- I prefer to write alone – other people's opinions are great and all, but I never really change anything according to their feedback

If any of the above hit a little close to home, it's likely that writing for you has a fair chunk of ego involved. Don't worry – that just happens to be the case with basically every writer that ever lived. The trick, however, is to really understand how your own ego and the need to defend it appears in your writing process.

It's OK to feel insulted and personally offended when someone doesn't like your work – but a skilled and competent writer has learnt to get over this quick so they can get to the important work of being better. Could they learn something from the criticism? If they didn't personally write this piece, what would they think of the assessment?

When you write, throw your heart and soul into the endeavor like your life depends on it. When you edit and evaluate a piece, though, take a big step back and become impersonal. A little cruel, even. This is the only way to stay vital and creative but also keep a good sense of perspective on how to improve.

An inconvenient truth

What I'm about to tell you now is an unpopular opinion and one you won't find in other writing guides. I've said above that if you are willing to accept criticism and move on, you get the reward of becoming a better writer. Abandoning your ego when necessary can lead to greater rewards and an enhanced competence as a writer. Fine and good.

But what if your original motivation for writing was no more complicated than, "I want people to praise me and to get glowing feedback. I want to be perceived as brilliant and smart and talented. I want to be popular." Now, I'm not saying that this Big Why is any less legitimate than any other. If this is your real reason, well, welcome to the club – like I said, writing is inherently narcissistic.

But it also means that you might choose to abandon writing altogether if it means you're signing up for more criticism and rejection than praise and glory. Many people have claimed to want to pursue writing because their friends and family have fed them encouragement. However, when they step out into slightly more hostile territory, and are asked to abandon the ego for a bit to do some hard work on their writing skills, they may suddenly find that writing isn't so fun after all, and that they are not in fact prepared to travel that route.

Again, this isn't necessarily a bad thing. Understanding and exploring your real motivations is always a smart thing to do. If you eventually learn that you'd rather write for friends and family or a small niche of people, there's nothing wrong with that. What doesn't make sense is signing yourself up for the sometimes grueling work it takes to improve as a writer if it doesn't actually tie in with your deeper motivation.

Chapter 6: Your Writing Workshop and Essential Hardware

Ok, so I promised that this book would not really be about the nuts and bolts of writing, but this chapter is an exception. In this chapter, we'll talk about creating a safe, productive and happy little writer's nest that you can work your magic in.

Your nest doesn't have to follow any rules other than those that will help you maximize your creative output. Most of the time, this will mean nothing more than removing distractions and interruptions to allow your natural creative spring to bubble up. Consider these elements as you set up a workspace that makes sense for you:

Concentration

You'll need a space that will allow you to do your thing without risk of pulling your energy away or putting any interruptions in your creative flow. For most people this means somewhere quiet and undisturbed, but some people also enjoy the quiet hum of a coffee shop or similar. Your place should allow you to follow a train of thought for as long as you want without distraction. Think about noise levels, other people coming to get you or things like Facebook or snacks distracting you.

Comfort

In a sense, discomfort is a kind of distraction that can pull your focus away from where it needs to be. Make sure that in your little nest, your physical needs are cared for and you are comfortable. Consider all your five senses and make sure you're treating each one right.

This means the room shouldn't be too hot, cold or draughty. Make sure your lighting is adequate, with a moderate source of preferably natural light coming from behind or to the side of you. Make sure there's enough airflow and fresh, clean air, and, obviously, make sure you're not wet or cold or somewhere dirty or untidy.

You can go full hippy with it and burn some special incense that gets your creative juices flowing, play whale music and light a candle, or you can head to a coffee shop you like and plug in your earphones while you type away with a cup of hot chamomile tea. Do what works.

If it's part of your process, buy a cheap printer (this is so you can print things out and do editing by hand with a series of pens and highlighters) and the literal files and folders you'll need to organize information. Some people like to have index cards stuck onto the wall to keep track of scenes/main ideas, other people use a whiteboard and coloured markers.

So, that's the hardware ...what about the software?

Most people find a word processer the best for writing, and use either Word or some notebook software on their laptop. There are some fantastic ones available that are very minimalist, to get rid of distractions and mimic that pure, white page in front of you.

Another idea is to get an app that cuts down on distractions (we'll look more at procrastination in, uh, a later chapter...) such as one that only allows you to look at blocked sites for a few minutes before cutting your connection and forcing you to get back to work.

Chapter 7: Setting up a Writing Community

Most beginner writers are like secretive moles working underground, writing alone at night where nobody can see them. But getting your work out there and in front of eyes other than your own is a vital, if sometimes painful, part of the process.

This is non negotiable.

If you think you can get away with not seeking the advice, support, opinions or feedback of others, think again. In fact, the more resistant you are to this idea, the more likely you are to benefit from it. It's not so bad!

Writing groups

I used to hate my writing group with a passion. Really. I would leave every week and secretly wish they'd all die of cancer. Sometimes I thought they were all ignorant, sometimes I got really angry with them, but occasionally, I felt like they had given me advice so valuable I don't know how I lived without it.

I'll say two things about writing groups: they are necessary, and just because you are occasionally uncomfortable with one, it doesn't mean that going isn't good for you. BUT another thing I'll say is that some writing groups are better than others, and that the whole process shouldn't be all pain and misery.

If you feel inspired at the end of your group meeting to hit the writing again, if you feel great but ready to try something new, you're probably with the right group of people. If you feel either elated that everyone thinks you're brilliant, or your soul is crushed and you feel like you can never write again, it's probably worth seeking out a group that will fit you better.

Writing groups where everyone is praised for whatever crap they put to paper (sorry) are not useful to anyone. If your group's mentality is, "everyone's a winner and nobody is allowed to offer any constructive criticism at all," your writing will not improve. Similarly, if your writing group is a den of snakes where a bunch of embittered writers take turns tearing each other down, your writing will also never improve.

You should find a group where each member is committed to improving, and where there is a culture of respect and mutual interest in growth. Follow your gut here and get away from groups dominated by fear, ego and narcissism. Also watch out for writing circles where the goal is not explicitly to improve but rather to share and chat. This ties in with the narcissism I mentioned earlier – again, it's not bad, but get stuck in a group like this and you'll feel grand but again, your writing will not improve.

Writing mentor

If you can find someone you admire and respect who is available to coach you on your writing directly, you have the chance to improve in leaps and bounds. But it becomes even more important here to be discerning. You should constantly ask yourself whether your involvement is leading to tangible benefits in your writing. Are you writing more? Are you improving on your weaknesses? Finishing projects and publishing them? Feeling inspired?

Online groups

The Internet thankfully gives you amazing access to other likeminded individuals and can be an excellent platform to elicit feedback and help. There are billions of forums, writing groups, blogs and mailing lists out there if you take the time to find them.

Again, you need to seek out that ideal balance between ego-stroking and critical enough to push you to be better. Anonymity can have its pros and cons. Consider carefully whether your online audience matches your final intended audience. Consider carefully whether your involvement with online groups is helping or hindering your overall output.

At the end of the day, a group is only as good as its effect on your writing. Your primary concern is not to feel good, to socialize or to promote yourself. It's to improve. As long as that's happening, how you choose to build your own writing community is up to you. But you do need a writing community!

Chapter 8: Give Your Writing a Heart

Right now, think of your favourite book.

Even if you have a few, what's the first one that springs to mind? Now, immediately ask yourself what emotion you attach to that book. You should be able to answer this quickly – in fact, you might have summoned up that same emotion merely by remembering that book. Long after the details of a particular book are forgotten, the emotion it stirred up still remains.

All the best books have this in common – they have an emotional core to them that really gives us a kick in the guts, one that we don't soon forget. A book can be interesting or novel or clever, but if it has this emotional depth to it, it will far and away win our attention.

How do you make use of this fact and inject some emotional relevance into your own work? Well, if you've taken the time to carefully consider your own Big Why, like we did in the beginning of this book, you're halfway there. Speak from your heart, from this Big Why, and your emotion and enthusiasm will naturally flow.

There are other ways to make sure you're giving your writing that compelling human touch, though. Consider some of these techniques:

- When you write, build in *natural tensions* to drive the plot. For human beings, everything in life is an epic battle between two opposing forces. Really. Love versus isolation. Good versus bad. Death versus life. Knowledge versus ignorance. All the best characters demonstrate a struggle between two fundamental and conflicting principles. All the best stories show an interplay between two viable but different life philosophies. Design your stories and characters around these conflicts and your writing will naturally be compelling. Think of fundamental human archetypes, of challenges and conflicts you face in life, of your own narrative. If it's interesting to you, it's probably interesting to others.

- Mean it. I know this sounds obvious, but don't write about something you actually don't care about. If you think, "well, vampires seem to be popular," your writing is not going to be convincing, and it will show. If it riles you up, write about it. Write about it like you mean it. If even you aren't sold, how do you expect to bring your reader around?

- Don't make things too perfect. Whether you're writing fiction or not, and whoever your audience is, don't make things too easy or neat. Leave some things unsaid. Don't underestimate your reader's ability to work hard to solve innate conflicts in your narrative. Be a little ambivalent. Don't solve all your problems all at once. After all – this is what life is like, right? Life is messy and strange and full of deep mysteries. If you want to emulate it, don't create work that is easy and overly simple.

- Don't hold back. Some of the best writing in the world was writing that was shocking, ugly or frightening. Also don't be afraid to explore lofty and idealistic themes in your writing. Go large. Push your boundaries. Be bold. Don't be afraid of being a little offensive, or unpredictable. When you're done with a piece of writing, look at it and ask yourself if everything's really on the page, or if you've unconsciously toned things down a bit out of fear.

- "Kill your darlings," as they say. Don't be afraid to let go of something if it isn't working. Be honest and ask if something is really fitting, if it's reaching your gut, if it feels authentic and if it's resonating. If not? Scrap it. It's

OK. The well is never empty. Keep writing and you'll get there.

Chapter 9: The Writing Habit

A friend of mine says they write no matter what. If there's a scrap of paper in their vicinity, it gets scribbled on. This friend's home is littered with millions of notebooks. Ask them why they write and they don't have an answer. "I just do."

This is fantastic. But, sadly, it's not good enough on its own.

What do I mean?

A writing compulsion is not the same as a writing discipline. Enjoying writing and seeking it out naturally is the first step, but it's not sufficient on its own to ensure that you're reaching your potential.

No, to fine tune discipline takes boring things like work, dedication and commitment. If you're one of these people that believes that writing is a thing you do almost by accident, when the muses smile on you and gift you a fabulous idea one day when you least expect it ...well, abandon that idea now.

Inspiration is fantastic, and when it happens, you should thank your lucky stars and squeeze whatever you can from it. The hard truth, though, is that life is mostly made up of uninspiring and regular-looking moments, a whole bunch of them, and if you hope to create something special, it's more or less up to you to do it.

Be realistic. Nothing in life happens in this fairy tale way. While a flash of artistic inspiration can certainly spur you on and act as a wonderful catalyst, even the most perfect creative gift from heaven is nothing without hard work to bring it to its full potential.

Here's the bad news: if you want to be a better writer, you need to write EVEN WHEN YOU DON'T FEEL LIKE IT.

Yes, let that sink in for a bit. Consider it a job. Consider it a life obligation on par with caring for your children or paying taxes. If you want to have any success of taking your writing to the next level, you'll need to work, and you'll need to work *hard*.

This means that for every happy moment when things fall into place and you look at an awesome thing you've made, there are twenty moments where you're staring at a horrible thing that doesn't work. For every paragraph that sings, there are forty paragraphs that thunk and clunk along and need to be thrown to the scrap heap.

Think about it: *most of your work as a writer is creating horrible writing.* Like someone sifting for gold, most of what you see every day is just plain old mud.

When you commit to being a writer and working hard on your craft, you are not committing to the shiny gold bits – that's too easy. What you're committing to is all the mud in between. Are you willing to work away at it, sometimes for days and days only to backspace the whole business and start again from scratch? Are you willing to write the same sentence over 20 times until it's what you want it to be? Congratulations, you have the temperament to be a writer.

So, how are you going to do the boring day-in-day-out work of writing? How are you going to put in your hours, your blood and sweat and tears?

- Decide on a daily time commitment and stick to it. For that time, you sit on your butt and work, no excuses. It doesn't matter if you produce garbage or manage only a few good lines after an hour. Just keep the channels open and keep going. Think of writing time as non-negotiable. Turn up at the page no matter what.

- Be regular. Make writing a literal habit. Find a place in your schedule and devote it to writing. Everything else can be shuffled.

- Set yourself goals. This could be word count goals, writing group meetings or some other metric that shows you are improving. Pencil in your diary some specific times where you'll stop and ask – is this working? Then adjust as necessary.

- Always, always, always have a notebook and pen around you for if you start leaking ideas anywhere.

- Make a promise to yourself to stop being self-deprecating about your project. Tell people honestly what you're up to and be proud. Don't undermine yourself or be bashful. They may even help you to keep accountable.

- Don't share your work willy-nilly with whoever wants to see it. People's opinions are valuable, but can be a disaster if injected into the process too soon. Get your say out, and know when to take your work for criticism in a *controlled* way. Nosy partners or family can kill a new work in progress – so keep your boundaries.

Chapter 10: Writer's Block and Why You Should Love it

I like to think of writing as a kind of therapy, and when you have writer's block, something interesting is usually going on. Don't freak out, don't rush in to try to figure out why you can't think of anything, just stop for a second and have a good look at where you are.

Writer's block can be a valuable tool if you're not afraid of it and know how to use it when it emerges. Feeling "stuck" can actually be a fantastic moment full of clues about how to proceed. The next time you feel dried up and unable to move on, ask yourself the following questions:

- Is there something on the horizon you're avoiding? Are you getting close to doing or writing something you're actually afraid of?

- Look at what happened immediately before you felt the writer's block. Do you always feel uninspired writing about a particular character or idea? Could this be a clue that this idea or character isn't working for you anymore?

- Think of the last time you bust out of writer's block and exactly what it was that got you going again. Can you recreate that now?

- Do you perhaps just need a break? If you've been going all out, heed the call and take a breather to rest and refresh.

- If you're bored …you might be making your readers bored too. It's hard, but it might be time to admit that your idea has run its course and isn't so engrossing as you first thought.

- Have you unwittingly allowed premature criticism of your work to block you? What I mean by this is showing your work to another person before it's really ready, and then unconsciously holding this person's opinion in your mind as you write. This can be a kind of performance anxiety.

- Maybe, and don't get a big head here, maybe what you're holding back from is the fear of success. Nothing can be so threatening to your idea of yourself as a bad writer than writing something amazing, right?

Chapter 11: Writing Myths

"I'm not talented enough to be a writer"

A little child doesn't need a scrap of talent to learn to speak and write, he only has to keep trying until he learns. You're kind of the same. Having a natural interest in writing and feeling drawn to keep going when it's difficult may be the thing people talk about when they talk about "talent", and for sure this is better to have than not ...but by far the biggest determiner of your success as a writer is your intention and the quality of the effort you put in. Period.

"I'm just going to work on this piece until it's finished and perfect..."

Nothing in life is ever finished and perfect, especially that paragraph you've been working on for eons. The irritating reality is that a lot of the time you have to settle for "good enough" or you'll drive yourself crazy. I believe it's a good sign if you look back on past work and cringe with embarrassment – it shows you're growing. Don't be one of those people who sits churning the same idea over and over in your head. Let it go, as it is, and let the fresh ideas come. Trust that you have more in you, and that you *will* improve if you keep going.

"Only crappy, lowest-common-denominator, poor quality stuff becomes popular, so why bother with working my masterpiece when I'll never make money from it?"

This one's complicated. Somewhere out there, a deeply intelligent, hard working and talented individual was working on an epic fan fiction novel that would have brought tears to the eyes of every mom that read it, just at exactly the moment that E L James started to make obscene amounts of money with *Fifty Shades of Grey*.

As grammar teachers and general humans with a scrap of common sense wept quietly, James laughed all the way to the bank. Why bother with finely crafted sentences and rock-solid plot and character when this buffoon could make millions with writing that would have made High School scribblings look like Dickens?

Firstly, a big part of this is merely an excuse. Seriously. The fact is that high quality, innovative content *does* make money, and *does* become popular. Do your best, and let it go. Secondly, it comes back to ego. Most writers out there feel a quiet rage and indignity at the fact that James won success when she's clearly an inferior writer. Whether she is or isn't is not my business to say (ok, she is!) but she was successful for a reason, and a savvy writer can put their ego aside and ask why.

James found a way to tap into something so immensely attractive that she created a storm in a readership that was unfamiliar with light BDSM erotica but, as it turns out, pretty keen to pay for it. While people heaped scorn on her for writing trashy "mommy porn" the fact is there is not much stopping *you* from doing the same.

James and people like her, in fact, show us that success is not some airy-fairy magic, but a real possibility when all the right elements are in place. It's true that publishing and the way that people consume media is changing faster than we can think about it, but this means that there are *more* opportunities, not fewer.

Never write something you don't believe in, or create something low quality because you think you don't have to – or shouldn't – try harder. Underestimating your audience is a fatal mistake. Put your heart, soul and sweat into writing something of value, and then release it.

"I'm a writer. I don't know about the marketing side of things and I don't want to. If I create a good book, people will come. Eventually. Probably."

Having said what I just did, it's important to note that in today's world, even the most perfect bit of genius needs help with visibility. It needs to be promoted. It needs to be *seen*. I had some trouble with this myself initially, but my hesitance was mostly due to fear. If you hope to make a success of your book, you *will* need to promote your book. You *will* need to create and nurture a readership/fan base and you will need to keep them happy by giving them what they want.

If you don't, you risk becoming one of the millions of "authors" languishing alone in corners of Amazon that nobody looks at, and nobody ever will. It sucks, I know, but it's the truth. To stand out in a sea of billions of people making noise, you'll have to make sure you have something interesting to say, but you'll also have to do your best to catch attention.

We'll consider this all in a later chapter, but it can be a rude awakening for many to discover that getting the damn book finished was actually the smallest of their worries. Finding an adequate platform to launch their work, winning and keeping admirers and marketing a brand that actually has any hope of making money – *that's* where the real slog comes in.

"I'm not unique enough!"

This is another tricky one. There are two sides. One the one hand, many respectable authors do quite well creating products that are more or less rehashes of the same old themes – and it's great! They know what works and their readers love it. There's nothing wrong with this. But on the other hand, finding success initially can be difficult if you don't bring anything new to the table. Established authors get to rest on their laurels a little, but it is true that if you want to snag some attention, you're going to have to be something special.

As far as this goes, I have no advice for you. I truly believe that if you've effectively tapped into your Big Why, if you've thought through themes, characters and ideas that are compelling and have taken the time to *work* it, you will come out with something that is truly, 100%, absolutely your own and nobody else's.

This book is about creativity. No matter how full the world is, trust that you can still think of new things. Believe that no matter how crowded the market feels, that you *do* have a perspective that is all your own. Don't stress about how novel you appear, spend that energy instead on trying as hard as you can to tap into your own perspective and exploit that to its fullest.

Chapter 12: More Nuts and Bolts: Creativity Exercises

On that note, I want to share a few ideas and techniques you can use to stimulate your own creativity and get your juices flowing. It's important, as you try each of these exercises, to stay open. Don't go into things with your mind closed before you've even started, making assumptions about what results you'll receive. Be playfully curious, and let things *emerge* rather than wrangle them out.

Exercise 1 – Shit Happens

If life were simple and easy, there would be no stories. Shit happens, if you'll pardon the expression, and plot is what happens in response. Give your characters a bit of grief. If you don't know where to take a story, ask yourself, what's the worst thing that could happen right now? What would seriously get in the way of my character getting what they want? The rest of the story will be figuring a way around that. In non-fiction, you can do this in the form of counter-arguments. Logically create a structure where two sides are "arguing" – it's more interesting if it's a close match!

To exercise this skill of building in tensions, go around today and brainstorm all the ways your life could go wrong. If you're sitting in a café, ask how the rest of the day would play out if you were suddenly beset by zombies. What would you do if you went home this afternoon and mysteriously found everything in your home missing, with nothing but a note written in Russian stuck to the bathroom mirror? What if an alien came out of your coffee mug and told you everything you believed about the world since you were a child is completely wrong?

Take your time with this. As you walk around, really relish the thought that a great story starts when, well, shit happens. Go over the top. What's the thing you care most about in any particular moment? Think of something to get in the way of that. Then, think of ways you could *resolve* that. How could you save and redeem things?

Exercise 2 – People are Multitudes

The following exercise will help you create real, compelling characters that will crawl out of your pages - if you're writing fiction, that is.

Start by thinking of someone you know well and have a strong reaction to in general. This could be a person you're close to, but it doesn't matter if you love them to death or want to strangle them ...to death. Take a moment to think of all the things that characterize this person's essence. You could do this by creating a mind-map or just sketching out a few words, phrases, images or symbols that capture their personality.

Now, imagine another person you know who is as different from this person as possible. This might even be you! If your first person is stubborn, head strong and deeply practical, think of a friend you have who is a loosey-goosey, fickle and a head-in-the-clouds type.

Ok? Now, put those two people *together*. It might be these people actually do interact in real life, in which case you have a lot to work with, but if not, try to imagine them together. What kind of conversations do they have? What kind of arguments? Literally picture the things they would say to each other and the attitudes and emotions that would emerge when such different people collide.

Picture our example people having a fight over how boring and predictable the one is, and the boring and predictable one taking the moral high ground because at least they have some goals in life, as boring as they are. Picture the conversations in detail.

Finally, take this dynamic, this dialogue and this tension and build it into a single character. All the best characters are a little conflicted. Nobody is all one thing or all the other. No, the best characters are complex, they change, and sometimes they don't make the most sense. Think of yourself. You may consider yourself as X, Y and Z ...but if you look a little closer, you also have a tiny little bit of the unexpected Q in you, too. There's also a little part of you that is *exactly the opposite of the rest of you.*

A lot of the time, compelling characters are believable because they are flawed in this way. A strong man is compromised by his weakness, the ignorant person in the story shows that they are the wisest of everyone, the pretty girl is revealed to have an ugly, mean streak, and the evil villain of the tale is revealed to have a hidden core of compassion.

When you sketch out your characters, always embed within them this tension. Make them 90% one thing and 10% the opposite. It's the tension that will originate plot and interest and excitement. And it's up to you to decide how you will let them solve this problem!

Exercise 3 – Translations

The only way we can ever communicate with each other is through symbols. Whether you do that through mathematics, through the written or spoken word, through images or facial expressions, or whatever, every form of expression is a *translation.* A lot of creativity is merely being skilled at as many different expressive languages as possible. For example, a good piece of fiction uses many and varied symbols and so gets its message across really effectively.

To develop the skill of expression in yourself, you need to be comfortable with making synonyms and metaphors, in other words the ability to say something in many different ways. This is particularly helpful in fiction writing.

To do this exercise, go about your regular day as normal. Only, whenever you encounter something, "translate" it. Examples will show what I mean. Let's say a colleague at work literally says to you the words, "this situation has to either change or end; I've had enough."

First, try thinking of different words to express the same thing. It's now or never. Adapt or die. I'm at the "end of my tether". Think of symbols to express this same sentiment. A rope being pulled between two people, one fiber away from ripping in half. What music goes with this idea? Shrill violins that show something is about to go bad very soon? Do you find yourself holding your breath?

What colours, shapes and symbols go with all of this? What *texture* is the concept of "now or never"? If this idea were a person, what would they look like or do? Put all of it together into a scene if you can. Can you see a rock climber, holding onto a cliff with his fingernails, dangling above a gaping abyss below, the scene swelling with dark clouds and foreboding drum music as it dawns on him – things have to change or end – he has to fix things now or it's over forever for him?

Obviously, you shouldn't space out and daydream when your colleague is talking to you if you can avoid it, but you get the picture. When you do these mental conversions, what you're actually doing is flexing your creativity muscles. I'm sure you've heard the old writing adage, "show don't tell," and this exercise is just the thing to teach you how to do that. The more channels you have at your disposal to express your big idea, the more effective your message will be – and the more colourful!

Do this occasionally as you go about your life (remember that bit about being a writer even when you're not writing?) and allow your brain to go loose and let in new ideas you've never considered before. Different themes, images and ideas will emerge, and you'll develop a richer sense of imagination that will give your writing depth and believability.

Exercise 4 – Dali's trick

This final exercise is a bit of wild card but personally one of my favourites. I have no idea whether it's true or not, but there is a rumour that Salvador Dali used this technique to generate some of the bizarre imagery so distinctive to his paintings. It goes like this: sit in comfortable chair with your arm dangling off the armrest, lightly holding onto a spoon. Just below, on the floor, place a glass saucer or plate that would catch the spoon should you drop it. You should also prepare a notebook and pen within easy reach.

Now, you lean back in the chair and try as hard as you can to fall right asleep. If you're lucky, images will bubble up in your unconscious mind as you gear up to start dreaming. Right about this time your grip on the spoon will loosen and you'll drop it, where it'll fall clattering onto the plate and wake you up. Before you even know what's happening, you reach for the notebook and scribble down whatever was in your mind at just that moment you were slipping off into dream world.

It sounds cheesy, I know, but I have frequently found insight and arresting imagery by plumbing my dreams for content. Do this carefully. You may even deliberately ask your unconscious mind while awake to work on a problem and then wait and see what your dreams throw up. You could choose to keep a dream journal beside your bed and write in it every morning before the ideas of the night past evaporate. You may well not come up with anything – but then again you might.

Exercise 5 – As Good as a Holiday

This is not so much an exercise as a way of life, and something you might consider doing indefinitely. The heart of a creative response to life, the root of creating things in this world rests in novelty. Creativity doesn't lie in your stale old routine or in the things you already know about. It's *out there*, new, fresh, and a little scary. It's something, by definition, that you haven't done before.

To get well acquainted with it, you need to get comfortable with newness, with taking risks and doing things you never have before. The more new things you try, the more channels you open for potential creativity to flow.

Do new things. Shun routine and stop making assumptions:

- Eat food you haven't eaten before. Try new recipes or strange food combinations. All the best sci fi writers, I'm sure, have put something bizarre on toast just to see what would happen.

- Listen to music you're not familiar with, watch TV and movies you find strange and branch out with your reading material. Act out of character and try something you thought you hated.

- Go travelling without any plan of where you're going. See places with fresh eyes and act spontaneously.

- Take up a new hobby that uses a completely unfamiliar skillset. Flamenco dancing, pottery or beat poetry may all be that special ingredient your writing could use.

- Try other art forms. Take up watercolour painting or do crafts to loosen any interesting ideas you may have hidden in your brain. When I say "art forms," I'm not excluding Play Doh sculptures or drawing smiley faces on lemons.

- Exercise – the blood flow is good for your brain and the endorphins will keep you resilient and productive.

- Dress uncharacteristically and practice expressing yourself out of what's normal for you. Why can't you take a risk and wear something you're a bit too shy to? Try a new scent, wear a colour you never do or buy something whimsical to wear.

Chapter 13: Effective vs. Ineffective Writing

Writing is a habit that you can develop just like you can develop other habits. This chapter is all about ineffective, inelegant and inefficient ways to write, and how you could remedy them to make better use of your time, energy and creativity.

Procrastination

Ok, here it is. Here's the section on procrastination.

The best thing you can do to kill this filthy habit is to understand *why* you do it. For many writers, procrastination is protective. You've convinced yourself you're not good enough, you're scared of failure, scared of the effort, and so you put it off with fantastic excuses so that eventually, you can look back and say, "see? I can't do anything."

If this is you, you need to start small.

Give yourself lots of opportunities to prove yourself wrong. Don't make grand plans, just give yourself assignments you know you can do. Write 100 words one day. Praise yourself. Write 200 the next day. Don't catastrophize if you fail, just ask yourself why and then get back on it the next day. 300 words. And so on.

A good technique is to just start. Promise yourself that no matter what happens, you'll at least sit down for five minutes every day, come hell or high water. What usually happens is you get stuck into it and want to carry on writing after all.

If you procrastinate because you're a lazy bastard, like me, then there's no way around it: you have to stop being a lazy bastard, and that's about all.

Choose your most productive time of day (for me, it's the morning) and then schedule your writing for then. Write no matter what. Tell others if their knowing would push you to write each day. Reward yourself if it helps. Say affirmations in the mirror, track your progress with an app or say a little prayer and remember your Big Why every time you feel like you'd rather watch TV and veg out than write.

It doesn't really matter what "tips and tricks" you use – at the end of the day, you either write or you don't. You either reach your goal, or you don't. This is not a motivational book (can you tell?) and I can't say exactly what will be the most inspiring thing for you, but I can say this: you *could* watch TV instead of write. You *could* put this off till tomorrow, or next week. Or, you could be better than that. Decide what you want and do it. There are millions of hopeful, unfulfilled authors out there who will never amount to anything, but there are zero authors who are successful who got there by watching TV and vegging out. The choice is yours.

Perfectionism

Do you notice how often people claim perfectionism as one of those "good vices" – you know, a bit like caring too much or being too handsome? Fact is, perfectionism is one of the *worst* habits you can have. Perfectionists often end up producing the least, and having the hardest time with criticism. Perfectionists never finish. At root, the perfectionist is driven by fear, and as long as that fear is in place, growth will be limited.

It takes courage to be in process. What I mean is it takes a lot of guts to look at yourself, *as you are right now*, and accept it. You may think you are motivating yourself by being harsh and having impossible standards, but what you are really doing is shutting yourself off from the very process that would actually make you better.

This is because failing is an intrinsic part of succeeding. The messy business of trial and error is actually the place where you learn to be excellent. If you're unwilling to dwell in that vulnerability and uncertainty – you don't learn, plain and simple. And so "perfection" becomes stubbornness, pride and stagnation.

Routinely tell yourself it's OK to mess up. In fact, *plan* to mess up. Reframing "mess ups" as your goal. Mistakes and imperfect attempts are really just a way to learn, and if you accept them for that, they're not so scary any more. Laugh at yourself a little. Shrug off looking like a fool – you won't die. Switch your goal temporarily from quality to quantity. Just write – you can edit and "fix it" later.

Disorganization

You wander, lonely as a cloud, and tumble into a quaint coffee shop that speaks to your heart. You sit down and curl yourself round a hot chocolate, taking out your Moleskin notebook and pink pen, ready to start the day's writing. You're distracted for the next 10 minutes thinking about whether to order cake and then your friend calls and you spend the 10 minutes after that having a chat. Then you remember that you actually have to be in town in an hour and a half and so you cut your dreamy writing session short. You've only written one line, but that's OK, these things can't be rushed. You'll try again that evening.

Except that evening, you're tired, and you realize that whoops! you left your beautiful notebook at the café. Your table is covered with quilting supplies anyway so even if you had your notebook you wouldn't have anywhere to sit and write. But you went to the café this morning, so that counts, right? The next morning you write "characters" at the top of a loose piece of paper and brainstorm some random ideas. You lose that paper the following day while talking to your friend on the phone again...

This, ladies and gentlemen, is disorganization, and it's not cute.

I don't mean to crush your artist's spirit, but at some point, you're going to need files. You're going to need a dedicated place to write and a space in your schedule that's cordoned off for this and nothing else. You'll need paper, mountains of it, and a way to organize it. You'll need files on your computer and they'll need to be organized logically, where you can get at them. You'll need a small notebook to carry with you and endless, endless pens.

Chapter 14: Writing Strategies That Work

Maintaining focus while writing

- If you don't already, start supplementing with Omega 3 fatty acids from fish oil or similar. Make sure you're getting adequate sleep at night and make sure you're doing what you need to keep any medical issues manageable. A diet rich in fiber, low GI grains and high quality fats (coconut, olive and macadamia nut oils, for example) will keep your energy levels stable and help you keep focused while writing. Stay hydrated and avoid too much caffeine, alcohol or sugar spikes – they'll give you a temporary boost but you'll pay later.

- Write for 20 minutes or half an hour and then get up to stretch, walk around, drink some tea or gaze out the window. Think of it as a periodic refresh to stop things from getting stale.

- Mix things up a bit – write in different locations or with slightly varying stimuli around you to keep your brain active and engaged. Write outside when the weather's good or occasionally write with a friend (if they're not chatty!) I like burning incense as I work as I find it pulls me back into the moment and gives my writing sessions a sense of ceremony. Try what works for you and enjoy it.

- Take up an auxiliary meditation practice – the skill of opening up still, aware moments within your day will benefit your writing enormously.

- Make sure you're exercising often. Disengage your brain completely at times and flood it with oxygen and endorphins – you'll feel fresh and strengthened when you return to the page.

Boosting productivity

- Of course, the golden rule is quality and not quantity, but if you're starting out you will need to ramp up your output gradually until you reach a good momentum. Give yourself small, incremental goals every day – increase your writing quota every day by 100 words until you find a comfortable pace.

- Be firm with friends and family who think nothing of interrupting you or don't respect the time and space you've carved out to do your writing. If you need to, have a serious chat in which you explain just how important it is that you are left 100% alone during writing time. Get a sign for your door, work when the kids are at school or work away from home entirely – do whatever you can to minimize disruptions to your flow.

- Write when you have nothing to say. Write when you don't feel like it. Be OK with putting pen to paper in the morning when things are dry and it looks like nothing's coming out. Trust that once you've warmed up a bit, things will flow again. Some people do "morning pages" as a ritual. Start out the day with putting down some "word vomit" first thing in the morning. It doesn't matter, just start writing and don't stop. Write anything. *Anything.* Do this for 10 minutes and then stop. Think of this as stretching your writing muscles for the writing jog ahead of you.

- If you're frequently distracted by Facebook or the Internet in general, get an app that cuts your access to certain sites during certain periods, or which will block access after a specified amount of time. Some writing apps allow you to write with nothing on the desktop except a blank page that cannot be closed until your writing session is over. Explore some of these to see if one of them can work for you.

Fine tuning your time management

- You are never too busy. Don't self sabotage by scheduling your writing time when you know you'll be busy. Choose your freshest, most optimal time in the day and schedule your writing for then. Writing when everyone else is sleeping (early in the morning or late at night) is a good and time-honoured trick, but do what works for you.

- Don't rely on the goodness of your own heart to motivate you to write. Have a schedule, *and don't deviate from it.* Plan it and respect the dates as though they were as important as your wedding date or an important job interview. In other words, something pretty serious has to happen to stop you from going.

- What's that, something serious happened? That's OK, life is tricky, I know. But make a plan. Work something out. Carry your notebook around with you and scratch a few lines even if you're stuck on a bus in traffic. Do a thought exercise while driving on your way to an impromptu meeting. Remember, writers are still writers even when they're not writing. Keep going, even if conditions temporarily become difficult.

- It's more important in the beginning to be regular than to be prolific. It's better to earn yourself a daily 20-minute writing habit that lasts for 2 years than to go big with 4 hours a day that lasts for a month and then never happens again.

Dealing with a lull in motivation

- Writing can feel like a long endless slog with no light at the end of the tunnel. When you're feeling spunky and motivated, write your future tired self a letter reminding them why you're doing what you're doing, and why they should keep going. Whip this out when you're low on energy and thinking of giving up.

- Try to tap into your Big Why any time you feel your enthusiasm waning. A drop in energy can hint at a place where you need to ramp things up or inject more feeling into your writing. If you're bored, write until you're interested again. Use your boredom as a rudder or a compass and adjust continuously. What would it take to get your interest again? Write towards that.

- Reach out to others. Often, a drop in motivation happens because we feel like we're trekking alone on our journey. Connect with other writers for some support, positive feedback or even some commiserating. You won't feel so alone and you may even learn a few new strategies for getting the stamina to keep going.

- Think back to some happy writing moments – moments where you were praised or recognized, moments where you were in the "zone" and writing effortlessly. Try to recapture what exactly was special about those moments – there are more in future if you keep going.

Chapter 15: The Editing Process

Here be dragons. Editing can be the cauldron in which you brew up your unfinished scratchings into perfect literary elixirs – or it can be a whole lot of bubble and trouble.

A good process is to have some sort of rough draft period where you write down what you need to without restraint. Give yourself the creative free-reign to just put pen to paper (or finger to keyboard) and get everything out. Write quickly and don't go back or pause to fix anything. The name of the game here is speed, and to get *volume*.

Once you're satisfied you've got it all out, it's up to you to decide where you'll take the editing process from there. There are a few approaches:

Write Fat, Edit Lean

The idea is to spew out a lot of words, and then go back later, picking through the rubble to find the gems. Your editing here is getting rid of the junk to reveal the good stuff hidden within. This is a good method if you like banging away a keyboard and like to build up a good momentum. Avoid this technique if you don't ever feel like you get a good rhythm going and don't get the impression you could just sit and write for 10 minutes solid.

Write Lean, then Plump It Up

The other way is to first piece together a skeleton and then go back later to fatten it up with "prettier" writing. I personally find this style less appealing, and I believe it may be more useful for non-fiction writing ...but it's really up to you.

Once you have your initial chunk and you're ready to do your editing, you also need to decide on your method. You could print things out with large font and generous spacing and then manually go through with a highlighter or red pen (this is fantastic and I love doing it this way) or you could simply do multiple "sweeps" over your text using the same word processor you wrote it in.

Some people like to print things out, then literally chop up the paragraphs and shift them around if part of their editing means changing up the order and pacing of events. Another good technique is to read it all aloud to find places where the flow is "sticky" and where you need to adjust punctuation. If it sounds good, it'll probably read nicely, too.

A good technique to do rather extensive editing is to go through the text with different coloured highlighters. Make marks on the paper depending on how you *feel* as you read. For example, use pink to make a mark the moment you start losing interest. Use green to show where you felt a little confused. Use yellow to show where you were reading faster because you were really excited about what would happen next.

This is a fun exercise to ask someone else to help you with – the kind of feedback you'll get from them will be far more useful than anything else they'll give you. Look at the response and ask yourself – why did they lose interest here? Are my sentences too long? Am I just repeating myself in this paragraph? Do this a couple of times with different people if you like.

You might like to take your editing process to your writing group, if they do that sort of thing. They will most likely only be able to give you general feedback ("I don't like the first person voice here") but it's a good start. Alternatively, hire a freelancer online to go through your work and give you feedback. It'll help if you ask them to answer specific questions for you:

- What part did you like best?

- What part did you like least?
- Can you find any grammatical errors?
- Can you find any spelling errors?
- Can you find places where the word choice or sentence structure can be changed so the meaning is clearer?
- What do you think about the length of the piece in general?
- What do you think of the tone?
- Is the "voice" correct and consistent? (i.e. first, second or third person)
- Are then tenses consistent?
- Are there any logical inconsistencies?
- Did you generally *like* the piece?
- Where the characters relatable, real and likeable?
- Was the argument, if there was one, persuasive?
- What would you change?
- Would you like to read more of the same? Why or why not?
- What do you think about the paragraph length and sentence length?
- Are there any overused words or expressions?

If you're eliciting the feedback and help from another person, be a grownup and be prepared for whatever they tell you. Make it safe for people to tell you the truth, or you're asking to be put in a bubble to protect your ego. Anonymous feedback is often the best for this reason – people have no incentive to lie to you. Thank the person for their perspective (even if it makes you feel bad) and use the information wisely. You're not compelled to change everything a person doesn't like, but try to be neutral and rational about it.

Finally, the editing process must, at some point, *stop*.

This is tricky because for the most part, you could go on forever if you wanted to. Don't expect to ever reach perfection. Don't expect a moment where you'll be so thrilled with a piece you can't imagine changing a single thing. But do try to reach a point where you know you've put in the work, where you're sure the message is there, more or less, and where you're happy to take the lessons you've learnt from it and move on.

Often, the real improvements come with the next piece, and in a sense, everything you write is a rehash of the same story you keep on telling throughout your life. The key is not to let obsession with the perfection of one piece keep you from working on other things, or sap your energy and self esteem to keep writing.

Many times, the temptation to tinker with something you've already written is just a procrastination technique to stop you from writing *something else.* Do your best. Work on it, a lot. Then know when to let go and try something else.

Chapter 16: Writing Blunders

And now, just for fun, let's look at a few all-too-common yet easily avoidable writing mistakes that even the seasoned pros make occasionally. It's the age of the Internet: I have no doubt that you can source obvious writing tips from literally anywhere, but I have nevertheless compiled a handy collection of those crimes I know are easy to commit – and how to avoid them.

As you work through your editing process, skim over these to make sure you haven't inadvertently made a writing blunder.

- Don't introduce the reader to a character by having them stare at themselves in the mirror or get dressed in the morning. It's boring and overdone. Put your character in a real life situation instead, to show their character.

- Don't date your work by referring to particular celebrities, the prices of things or Internet memes. Ask yourself if a reference to a song or product will hold up in 2 years or so. If not, drop it.

- It goes without saying, but if you're writing sex scenes, be very, *very* careful about your tone. Unless it's obviously erotica, avoid rude slang and expletives and leave most of if to your readers' imagination. Trust me. A good rule of thumb is to avoid writing about sex at all in regular fiction.

- It's dead basic, I know – but make sure you're actually formatting paragraphs correctly. They should all be of roughly the same length, contain a topic sentence and have one idea per paragraph.

- Choose a spelling convention – American or British – and stick to it.

- Avoid making your characters speak in over-the-top slang/vernacular. It's tiresome to read someone spelling out an accent, and can even be offensive. Throw in a little here and there if you want, but try to show character, ethnicity and social class in other ways.

- I'll say it again: show, don't tell. Never write something like, "he was furious." Instead, use your words to tell the reader about the exact red colour that went to his face and the vein that throbbed in his temple. Exercise 3 above is great for this.

- Try to avoid second person voice. This involves writing things like, "You wake up to the smell of burning gas. You wonder what's burning..." Although it can be a great way to create an immediacy and intimacy in writing, it's not really suited to longer works and can be hard to get right. Most of the time, you can achieve the same result in more conventional ways.

- Avoid the "as you know, Bob" mistake. This is when you get your characters to explain to the reader what's going on, although to another character who would reasonably know it already. Think, "Oh, brother, ever since our mother died, you know I've been a little distant, and when we sold the farm last year it was worse..." Again, show instead of tell. Put clues here and there – your reader will figure things out for themselves.

- Don't have a crush on your characters. This might seem funny to some people, but it's actually pretty common. Don't launch into a description of a character that sounds like you're a stalker admiring every mole and freckle. It's a convention in some genres of romance to make the hero and heroine impossibly hot, but in all other writing, this is to be avoided. Regular people are more believable and relatable.

- Don't waste words and time on boring details. Begin scenes in the middle of action, rather than making the reader wade through a character arriving at a coffee shop and faffing around for 10 minutes before his friend arrives and the juicy dialogue begins. Don't bother telling about the little actions they do, unless they're applicable somehow. Your reader will fill in the gaps – focus on what's important.

- To make your dialogue authentic, read it aloud. Resist the urge to make characters grandstand and give soliloquys about your personal views. Believable dialogue is more fragmented.

- Don't be clever and try to change up the standard "dialogue tags" *he said* and *she said*. They're good enough on their own, I promise, and will be invisible to most readers anyway. Try being fancy and saying, "she explained" or "he wondered" and it only looks clunky. Instead, try to embed those meanings into the quoted words themselves, or use punctuation (! Or ?) to communicate the way someone spoke.

- In the same vein, kill adverbs. I love adverbs, and it's my greatest failing in life. Sometimes I catch myself thinking, "maybe I can just put an adverb in here…" but then I stop myself. Ask if there's not a *verb* you can use instead. Kill adverbs and reincarnate them as noble verbs. If you really can't, default to an adverb or nothing at all. For a very simple example, don't say "she put her glass down loudly on the table," say "she slammed her glass on the table." And so on.

- Keep variety in your sentence length. Keep a mix of long and short sentences. Those with the same length over and over and over again can be so boring they almost hypnotize the writer. Short sentences grab attention. Long, languid ones slow the tension down and ask the reader to wait a while…

- I know it goes without saying, but if you're bad at this, be extra extra doubly sure that you're not making common grammatical mistakes (you're vs. your for instance, or principal instead of principle) and be careful with easy-to-make errors like "I could care less" or "for all intensive purposes."

- Don't put two punctuation marks together. Ever!!

- Don't write for nothing. After reading a scene, paragraph, chapter, whatever, something must have *changed* somehow. There must be some kind of development. Before you begin writing it, ask yourself what the point of that part is – to show a change in the character? To reveal new information? If you haven't actually succeeded in doing that, scrap the paragraph entirely.

- Make sure you're not over using some words. Whip out your thesaurus. Word processors will let you search for every instance of a particular word. Don't use "giggle" or "bright" or say how a character "shot back" in dialogue every few lines. Mix it up.

- When naming characters, don't spend half a year pondering on the perfect name as you would your own child. It's incredibly awkward when a name seems like something fanciful and over-the-top, just to tickle the author. Long, unpronounceable names can be incredibly alienating – the reader will often skip over it mentally and lose that connection with them. This is bad especially if you have a lot of characters. Use an online random name generator or go through the phone book for natural sounding names, unless you're writing fantasy or something similar. Avoid "stripper names" ("Melody Lovemore", "Trixxie Jones", "Brandi Griffyn") …unless, you know, you're writing about strippers.

Chapter 17: A Step-by-step Process for Handling Rejection With Grace

First things first: rejection *will* happen.

You may be one of those people who think they'll just sidestep the whole nasty business by never showing their work to anyone, but I hope I have convinced you so far that that's not an option if you take your writing seriously.

But in showing your work, you open yourself to criticism, and you are made vulnerable to the awful, terrible, no-good feelings that come with being rejected. A good way to make sure you handle it well is to be prepared for it before it even happens. Here's a step by step process that I can suggest that will help you get a handle on the icky emotions and give you a way to squeeze the most out of the experience.

Rejection is an opportunity to learn and be better, and a great attitude is where you actually *want* and anticipate rejection. I'm not suggesting you become a masochist, but merely take a different perspective. Stephen King explained how he gleefully pinned all his rejection letters on the wall of his office, collecting them by the dozen and papering the walls of the very room he worked in. It wasn't some sick way to belittle himself (or maybe it was, Stephen King is a strange man) but a way to cultivate resilience.

Step One: Don't React Immediately

The first thing most people do when they are criticized is fight back. This makes sense. You perceive an attack (in this case, an attack to your self worth, to your identity and all the rest) and your instinct is to defend and protect yourself. You may get angry. Hurt. Miserable.

The problem is, criticism is not quite an attack, and so responding like it is will ensure you miss the learning opportunities hidden within it. Resist the urge to argue, even if you're only doing it quietly to yourself. I know some people who respect and admire their friends, but the second one of those friends says an unflattering word about their writing, they instantly take this as proof that the friend isn't as great as they thought they were. They instantly demote that person's opinion and taste, instantly try to neutralize the "attack" by invalidating the feedback they receive.

We all do this, and we all suck because of it. The first and best thing you can do when you are criticized is to stop and get a control of your emotions, gaining composure before you do anything else. Withhold on making a judgment. Don't jump to conclusions and say, "well, who is he to judge – have you read *his* stories?"

Watch for the temptation to snap back at another person, or to coolly write off their criticism because, well, what do they know? Simply hear the message, thank the person for their opinion and shelve it. They may be right, they may be wrong. You will only be able to appraise their criticism properly when you are feeling calm and levelheaded.

Take a moment to scream and cry into your pillow, put on a stop watch and give yourself 5 minutes to wallow and be the poor maligned misunderstood artist – but then get over it. Shake it off and move on to step two.

Step Two: Evaluate the Criticism

Once you've gotten the nasty feelings out of your system, or at the least sectioned them off to deal with in a more appropriate way some other time, it's time to look carefully at the data you've just received. I'm suggesting that you be clear headed and open to the criticism you receive, but I'm not saying you can't get feedback that is completely worthless. I'm not saying every bit of criticism you receive is worth the same and deserves the same consideration.

The next thing you have to do is ask yourself, as honestly as you possibly can, if there is any truth in the feedback. If somebody says, "your work is hard to follow and confusing at times," then your job is to go to your work and look with honest eyes to see if they're on to something. If they say something like, "I just didn't like this, it's not really my cup of tea," then you can shrug and move on with life. Not everyone has to like you or what you make.

If you look hard at your work and can admit that yes, the criticism may actually have a basis in reality ...excellent! You can thank the person *again* for uncovering this new aspect for you. Truly, they've given you something more valuable than a hundred "good job" comments. This is something you can work with. With this gift, your writing can become better.

The most likely outcome of this step is that you will look at your work and see a mix – maybe there's *some* truth in what has been said, but it's not the whole story. In this case, you suspend your judgment and wait till you have more data. If ten people tell you your work is confusing, take the hint. If only one ever does, you can be a bit more confident in writing that off as their problem. It's your call – but it's a call you can only make when you drop any ego and look at the situation rationally.

Step Three: Adjust and Repeat

Don't keep throwing your work at people who routinely say they don't care for it. Don't spend years of your life and valuable self esteem writing to people who can't and don't want to listen to what you have to say. Likewise, don't keep asking for feedback from people and never doing anything about what they tell you.

Feedback and criticism is valuable if something changes because of it. Let the process be dynamic and intelligent. You are not a performer on a stage pandering for attention or likes on social media. You're an artisan, and you need to keep working on your craft until it's the best it can be.

Take feedback to heart, make changes that you believe in and then seek feedback again to compare. Remember, you don't have to agree with the response you get. But give the process its due diligence. If you feel pressured to go one way and really want to go the other, there's only one solution: go your way and then see what happens. Even if you never get feedback from another human being, the world itself will be your critic and let you know how you did. If you enjoy writing something, have people who enjoy reading it and even make money from it, what could be better?

Things To Remember When You're Feeling Rejected

- Don't be tempted to think, "everyone is special, we're all great in our own ways, my work is just not appreciated right now for some reason..." I mean it. This kind of thinking will make you feel better in the short term but is toxic in the long term. Yes, *it is possible for you to write something crappy.* And it's OK! Write badly, it's not the end of the world. Don't be the kind of person who looks at shoddy writing and shrugs and says, "well that's just the honest expression of where I am in my artist's journey..." or whatever. No. There is good writing and there is bad writing. Strive to write well, but don't be horrified about writing poorly. Oh, you wrote something awful? So what? Look at it, admit it's *bad*, and move on.

- Everyone fails. Everyone turns out truly embarrassing, ugly, headache-inducing writing at times. In fact, I would suggest that even your favourite authors in the world have some dirty secrets you don't know about. It doesn't matter though. What matters is that they had the spirit and courage to keep going and get closer to the good stuff.

- The key to being resilient is not to give a damn. If you ever catch yourself censoring what you have to say because you are worried about what people may think, try think of it this way: imagine yourself on your death bed, at the end of your life. That's it, it's over for you. Have you got some untold stories you didn't get out while you had the chance? Have you hidden from the world the very things that made you special? Have you bitten your tongue and are now going to your grave never knowing what would have happened if you had the guts to speak up and be seen...?

- Remember that sometimes, critics really are just frustrated artists themselves. Trust your gut on this. It's so easy for someone who hasn't taken the chance to be vulnerable and expose themselves to pass judgment on someone who has. Take it for what it's worth. Sometimes, people will be mean because unconsciously, they are jealous that you're doing what they don't yet have the courage to do. Be kind to them and move on. You may inspire them to take the leap themselves one day.

- Rejection gets easier the more you do it. And you may as well get used to it, because as long as you're writing and putting stuff out there, there will someone with something to say about it. Grow a callous and accept that criticism and rejection are just part of the deal.

- If you're floundering and feeling bad about your competence, it may help to remember the praise you've received. Balance out any catastrophic thoughts you may have by remembering that although you've written something less than fabulous, there have been times when you've hit the mark perfectly. Keep going and you'll find those sweet spots again.

- Try to separate out your worth as a person from your skill as a writer. This can be tricky. Have the balls to feel great about yourself no matter how you perform. Remember to tell yourself that you're still a writer, you're still a good person and that you still have permission to keep writing!

- Lastly, treat positive feedback the same way: be neutral about it and evaluate it carefully. Are people just flattering you? How astute is their commentary anyway? Don't let these judgments disturb your core values and stay calm – appraise positive comments just the same as you would the negative ones.

Chapter 18: What About a Ghostwriter?

You know, I understand if you have a good, hard look at your life and think to yourself that honestly, you just can't be bothered. Maybe you really don't have the time. Maybe you've tried to improve but your writing is just atrocious and that's the end of it. Maybe you hate writing or English is not your first language.

Even still, though, I believe you should write your own work.

Why?

There are ghostwriters out there who are talented, hardworking and just the kind of people who will take your grand ideas and spin them into something special, without all the effort of, you know, writing it out yourself. With enough money, in fact, you could actually just *buy* yourself a good novel, put your name on it and call it a day.

Many "authors" do this, and if you're a fan of any famous bloggers, self help writers or other sundry famous folk, there's a good chance what you read was actually written by a ghostwriter. I'm not about to tell you what I think of the ethics of this (I think it's fine) and I'm not about to tell you whether you should go for one (you can) but I am going to say one thing.

Ghostwritten work is missing a crucial ingredient. It's something that you can't actually pay for, even if you had the money. It's not something you can describe to a freelancer you've never met and tell them to whip it up for you in a few weeks. Throughout this book, we've been going round and round this idea of creativity, this beautiful, elusive quality, this *thing* that makes dead words on a page come alive. I've tried to suggest ways you can cultivate this in yourself, ways to coax out this magic in ways that make sense for you, and ways to nurture it when you find it so that your writing is vibrant, human and completely captivating.

Ghostwritten work can be good. It can *very* good. But it can never capture this magic. Not even close. I'll be blunt to make my point: in the same way as you wouldn't expect to find love and romance with a prostitute, you can't expect to find personal, high quality and unique work merely by paying a ghostwriter.

Now, if the work you are commissioning is merely a how-to book, a compilation or guide, something light and silly, or, I don't know, a recipe book – it will be less obvious. Here, I would say go ahead and save yourself the trouble by hiring a professional and carrying on with the rest of your life.

But if you have a tender, special idea you've been nurturing for a while, yearning to grow it up into a big strapping book that people will read and be moved by – then *don't* go for a ghostwriter. They can craft you a convincing replica of what you tell them, sure, but it will lack the soul and punch that a book you wrote yourself would have.

There won't be the same level of conviction present in a book written by somebody who's approaching the thing as more of a technical exercise. Your efforts may even be a bit rougher, a little less polished and a little less sophisticated than theirs – but it will be *authentic*. And readers respond to authenticity.

Chapter 19: Launching Your Work

Once you've actually written the thing, you're going to need to find people to read it and hopefully, with a bit of luck, love it to death. The topic of how to promote, market and sell your work is massive and beyond the scope of this book, but we'll consider here briefly the elements you'll need in place.

Ideally, you'll start marketing your book before it even exists. If you're one of the many informal, unpublished authors who want to make a name for themselves on their own steam, you'll need to have a good idea of how to self publish.

The Internet has made all aspects of publishing – from the writing to the promotion to the actual exchange of money – easier and more accessible than ever before. Truly, someone today can write a book, design the cover, format it for Kindle, promote and sell it on Amazon or other platforms and collect money from sales directly – all without the help of anyone else.

But it's daunting. The real work of self-publishing is far, far greater than merely putting the book together, but consider the following questions to help guide your consideration for how you'll actually publish your baby:

Will You Self Publish At All?

First decide if you'll pitch to agents or publishing houses or go it alone and publish your book on a platform like Amazon. The former may never work out and may take a lot of stress and rejection, but still retains something of a gold standard in terms of the prestige of having a house's name behind you; the latter is less prestigious but more realistic if you really want the work out there and money in your pocket.

How Will You Cultivate An Online Presence?

This has gone from something that authors could optionally do to something mandatory. Authors these days are expected to be masters of self-promotion, so think of how to get your name and brand out there. A blog? A website with promotions, teasers and special discounts? A Twitter feed? A podcast? You could hire someone specifically to help with the promotion of your book or you could use any of the billions of marketing resources out there to piece together a campaign of your own. But it needs to be done, and it needs to be done *continuously*.

Who Is Your Audience, and How Can You Connect With Them?

Your audience should already be built into your work, and you should already have a firm idea of your demographic before you begin writing. But also brainstorm ways you'll form actual relationships with them, rather than just market your book in their general direction. How will you get feedback and requests from them? How will you reward their loyalty? What else does your audience want and how can you give that to them?

What Is Your Brand?

I know some aspiring authors are repulsed by the idea of marketing themselves and their work like a brand, but it needs to be done. Chat to a marketing expert or consult some literature on putting together a coherent image that you can communicate to potential readers. Try to really understand the market you are entering. Work alone or with a graphic designer to put together logos and book covers that are professional and consistent. Cultivate *yourself* as the creator of all this. What image do you wish to convey? What do you offer readers that they can't get anywhere else?

How Will You Price Your Work?

Will you write millions of short, serialized pieces that sell for nothing on Amazon and hope that in bulk, they'll amount to good exposure and a tidy profit? Or are you going to write longer, more quality pieces less frequently and charge more for them? Both strategies are valid. Do research on optimal lengths and prices for things, factoring into it the effort you've put in. One book will not be enough. Will you need multiple personas? A pseudonym? Will you launch on multiple platforms or just one? Will you offer initial discounts or a free run to get people interested?

What Can You Do Consistently To Maintain Your Marketing Campaign?

You'll be working your butt off to promote a new book, but it doesn't stop there. Decide upfront what level of engagement you're comfortable with *for the long term.* Can you maintain a blog for the next three years? A Twitter account? Will you hire someone to do it for you?

Ultimately, the best way to start with publishing yourself is to just do it. Just start. It will be inelegant at first, and your first attempt may very well bomb, but it's good to just start, and begin sooner rather than later to learn the hands-on lessons.

Through trial and error you can gradually build something effective and all your own. Self-publishing is a lot like being an entrepreneur: you learn by doing. Fail early and fail small, and you'll arrive more quickly at the place you want to be eventually.

Conclusion

And so, we arrive at the conclusion, although a writer's life, to be dramatic for a moment, is never really concluded. There are no easy answers, no quick hacks and tips. No shortcuts. But it is my hope that with this short guide, I have spoken to something in you, or at the very least, that you have disagreed with me enough to be spurred into action.

The creative process is possibly one of the most rewarding things in life. It's also a treacherous journey – sadly, many people never fulfill their real potential as writers.

This book has tried to focus on some of the earlier, less examined aspects of the journey – the urge to create at all, and how you can harness that and use it make your writing more powerful and effective. Wherever your journey as a writer takes you, I hope that the ideas in this book have convinced you to go a little further, and a little deeper with your message.

On to new beginnings.

And finally, I would love to hear if this book has helped you in any way. Leaving a very simple, one-sentence review for this book will only take 30 seconds of your time. But in doing so you would give me an invaluable insight as to how I can improve it and make it even more relevant to you, the reader. Without your support I couldn't be doing what I'm doing.

Clicking or typing in http://www.amazon.com/Simeon-Lindstrom/e/B0oLHUJSAK/ will take you to my author page where you can leave a short review for this book.

I have also listed a free preview of my other books in the last section of this book, so feel free to keep on reading.

Additional Writing Resources

A handy, random name generator:
http://random-name-generator.info/

"The Elements of Style" is a classic that never stops being relevant:
http://www.amazon.com/The-Elements-Style-Fourth-Edition/dp/020530902X

Try these fun writing prompts from Reddit:
https://www.reddit.com/r/WritingPrompts/

The indispensible 2015 Writer's Market:
http://www.amazon.co.uk/2015-Writers-Market-Trusted-Published/dp/1599638401

Possible freelancing sites to get logos, formatting, book covers and editing:
https://www.upwork.com/
https://www.fiverr.com/
https://www.freelancer.com/

Everything you need to know about self-publishing on Kindle:
https://kdp.amazon.com/help

Other Books by This Author

Self-Compassion - I Don't Have To Feel Better Than Others To Feel Good About Myself: Learn How To See Self Esteem Through The Lens Of Self-Love and Mindfulness and Cultivate The Courage To Be You

The world is a vast, complicated and sometimes downright hostile place. Today, more than ever, human beings have had to learn new ways to be resilient, know themselves and have the courage to be who they are. Our hyper connected world bombards us with images of phenomenally successful celebrities together with the expectation that we should want nothing but the best for ourselves at all times. But in a bustling world of 7 billion people, carving out a meaningful niche for ourselves can be daunting to say the least.

It's understandable that people feel the need to bolster their self esteem. Faced with millions of glossy images in the media about how we should live our lives, some have turned to trying even harder still to keep up. Others have merely given up. It's no exaggeration that people in the 21st century live in a world of infinitely more possibilities than any generation before them. We have experts and gurus of all stripes telling us that the life we have now is nothing compared to what we could achieve – and yet, we're as depressed and lacking in confidence as ever.

Self help books on the market today will tell you one of two things: either that you are perfect already as you are and needn't worry, or that with just a little (well, a lot) of effort, you *can* reach those goals. Be the best, smartest, most successful, thinnest and relentlessly happiest version of yourself possible. No excuses!

This book takes a different approach to self esteem altogether. If you're feeling overwhelmed and worthless, inundated with information, struggling to juggle life, expectations, and disappointments... it may be time for a little self-compassion.

Unlike self esteem or an inflated confidence level, self-compassion is a different way of looking at yourself and others, warts and all, and a way more realistic acceptance of the way things are. With self-compassion, you become unflappable, calm and self-assured - without the risk of narcissism or becoming self-absorbed. Through a series of exercises, this book will suggest a new, gentle yet extremely powerful attitude shift that can end feelings of self-hatred, doubt, shame and low self-worth forever.

Download this book and continue reading by clicking <u>here</u>, or visit http://www.amazon.com/Simeon-Lindstrom/e/B00LHUJSAK/

How To Stop Worrying and Start Living - What Other People Think Of Me Is None Of My Business

Stress is a lot like love – hard to define, but you know it when you feel it.

This book will explore the nature of stress and how it infiltrates every level of your life, including the physical, emotional, cognitive, relational and even spiritual. You'll find ways to nurture resilience, rationality and relaxation in your every day life, and learn how to loosen the grip of worry and anxiety. Through techniques that get to the heart of your unique stress response, and an exploration of how stress can affect your relationships, you'll discover how to control stress instead of letting it control you. This book shows you how.

But this book is not just another "anti-stress" book. Here, we will not be concerned with only reducing the symptoms of stress. Rather, we'll try to understand exactly what stress is and the role it plays in our lives. We'll attempt to dig deep to really understand the real sources of our anxiety and how to take ownership of them. Using the power of habit and several techniques for smoothing out the stressful wrinkles in our day-to-day lives, we'll move towards a real-world solution to living with less stress, more confidence and a deep spiritual resilience that will insulate you from the inevitable pressures of life.

By adopting a trusting, open and relaxed attitude, we'll bring something more of ourselves to relationships of all kinds. This book will take a look at dating and relationships without stress and worry, as well as ways to bring tranquility and balance into your home and family life. Again, this book is not about eradicating stress from your life forever. We'll end with a consideration of the positive side of negative thinking, and how we can use stress and worry to our advantage.

We will address physical, emotional, relational, spiritual, and cognitive and behavioral symptoms of stress.

And while most stress-management solutions offer relief for symptoms in only one or two of the above areas, this book will show you how all five areas are important, and a successful stress solution will touch on each of them.

Download this book and continue reading by clicking here, or visit http://www.amazon.com/Simeon-Lindstrom/e/B00LHUJSAK/

The Minimalist Budget: A Practical Guide On How To Save Money, Spend Less And Live More With A Minimalist Lifestyle

What's the first thing you think of when you hear the word "budget"? It's a meager little word, one that all too often comes after "tight". Maybe you think of this word as an adjective, something to describe a cheap and substandard car or hotel. "Budget" brings to mind rationing, a kind of money diet. If you're like many people, budgeting is something you do with a kind of deflated spirit: budgeting means bargain bin quality and the sad sense that what you want is going to be just out of reach.

This book will try a different approach to budgeting all together. It's a pity that the idea of living within one's means should be experienced as such a deficit – this book will try to show that when you apply the principles of minimalism to budgeting, you are neither in a state of self-denial or trying to survive a financial scrape. In fact, a minimalist budget is a particular approach to abundance and fulfillment that may seem counterintuitive to most.

Undoubtedly, what came into your mind when you heard the word "budget" was simple: money. Money is a thing to be feared, to be saved, to be celebrated when it's there and mourned when it isn't. Budgeting, we are told, is necessary. When you live in a world where there is always one more thing to buy, being cognizant of the fact that you don't have endless resources is just the practical thing to do.

However, budgeting can be much more than this. To put it simply, money is only *one* of the resources that we should be managing in our lives, and possibly not even the most important one.

As humans, it is our lot to deal with being finite beings: we have only so much time to spend on this earth, only so much time that we are allotted each day, only so much energy that we can give away before we run into a deficit.

In a sense, the principles of minimalism rest on a more fundamental interpretation of "budget". Just as you need to match your financial expenditure with your income, minimalism encourages us to match our needs with our actions. It doesn't make sense to buy food for 12 when you have a family of 4 in the same way it doesn't make sense to clutter up your home with things you don't want, like or need. Trimming away at unessential elements in your day-to-day life is an exercise in budgeting and minimalism both, whether you are trimming away excess expenses, destructive thoughts or junk in your spare room.

This book will offer an expanded notion of what it means to budget. We'll look at how money is not the only resource that needs to be managed, and a "life budget" that acknowledges your emotional, behavioral, social and even spiritual capital is more likely to lead to smarter decisions.

Minimalism is not, of course, about starvation or punishment. It's not about doing with less than you need. Rather, minimalism is about finding what you need and fulfilling that need exactly, without excess. It's a subtle point and one that the average person who has grown up in an industrialized capitalist society can miss: *to have exactly enough is not suffering*. Budgeting is therefore about understanding what you need to have enough, and how best you can allocate your resources to that end.

Most of the budgeting advice out there will come firmly out of the scarcity paradigm – you're usually offered a few ways to shave off money here and there. You are asked to look at all the instances where you are not spending or living on the bare minimum, and usually anything extra is framed as unnecessary, indulgent or, depending on who you talk to, bordering on immoral. These tips will tell you that after enough cheap toothpaste, homemade laundry soap and clothes bought out of season, you'll save enough money and make it all work. You're asked to look over your life and find places where you could manage, without too much discomfort, to do with less or even without.

While thriftiness and being money-conscious are excellent skills to have (and for some, absolutely necessary), minimalist budgeting is more about conscious decision making and less about stinginess and trying to endure a lack.

To show the difference, consider a purchase someone might make: a new dishwasher. On paper, the initial cost of a dishwasher might make it look like a kind of luxury. After all, you can simply wash the dishes *for free* yourself, right? In traditional budget land, a dishwasher may fall well into the category of "unnecessary". Can you do without it? Of course. Then, it doesn't belong in your pared down budget. On the face of it, this logic seems sound. In fact, while you're laboring away washing dishes by hand, you may even get the impression that doing it all yourself is kind of noble.

The "minimalist budgeting" in this book will ask you to take a more expanded view of the dishwasher. Not buying one will certainly result in less of your money spent. But, as mentioned, since money is not your only resource, by focusing on only this aspect you're not getting the full picture. Is the cost of doing dishes by hand *really* free? In your budget, have you factored in the fact that washing dishes saps hours of your life each week and makes you grumpy? If you're so wiped out at the prospect of another 45 minutes of housework at the end of the day that you give up and splash out on expensive restaurant food, you haven't even saved money, anyway.

When you lay alone in bed at night and ponder your existence, which will mean more to you: the extra cash you saved by not buying a dishwasher, or the lifestyle you gave up as the person who never has to worry about dishes again? You can't take your possessions with you when you die, they say, but which will be more soothing to you on your deathbed - the fact that your life was thrifty or that it was enjoyable and meaningful?

Simple budgeting doesn't take these kinds of things into account. The primary purpose of your life, at least in some sense, is to be happy. Money usually facilitates this. But if you're maximizing your money to the point that it makes you less happy, your budget is no longer serving its purpose. Minimalist budgeting is like regular budgeting, only with an eye to what is truly important. While this book will certainly show you nifty ways to save a buck here and there, it will also regularly ask you to examine what that buck means to you at the end of the day.

We'll explore shopping and spending habits, identify problem areas, think about debt and make achievable goals for home, work and more. We'll look at concrete ways to put some of these principles into action, and look at resources that will keep you focused and motivated. But at the same time, this book is also about the philosophy of minimalism, not thriftiness. If you can pair your budget plan with a more nuanced understanding of your relationship with money and how it ties into how you want to live, the changes you make will be more authentic and longer lasting.

Download this book and continue reading by clicking here, or visit http://www.amazon.com/Simeon-Lindstrom/e/B00LHUJSAK/

Love Is A Verb - 30 Days To Improving Your Relationship Communication: Learn How To Nurture A Deeper Love By Mastering The Art of Heart-To-Heart Relationship Communication

Have you ever noticed how often people say they wish they could "find" love? As if love were something beautiful to just stumble upon on the side of the road. Yet when you speak to happily married couples, especially those that have been married for decades, they never ascribe their success and happiness to luck. Instead, they'll probably tell you that a good relationship takes work - lots of it - and the continued effort and maintenance from both sides.

Love is a *verb*.

It is not something only some people are fortunate enough to catch and then merely set aside. It's not a prize you win or a box to tick on your life's checklist. Instead, love has to be kindled and rebuilt *every day*; it has to be invited in, nurtured, cultivated. Love is not something passive that you simply have or don't have - it's an active process and the continual expression of what's in your heart, mind and soul.

In this book, love is not a noun. It isn't some mysterious gift from the gods that falls into our laps, but something that we can work on and build with intention. So, in that spirit, this book will not be a dispassionate list of relationship advice, or theories about the way people work together, or tips to heat up your sex life.

Instead, this book will ask you to become *actively* involved, to not just read but to constantly apply what has been read to your own life. And since we are on the topic of heart-to-heart communication, you're naturally going to need to rope in your partner, too. The exercises are experiential, meaning, simply, that you have to actually *do* them in order to benefit from them.

You'll be asked to be honest with yourself, get out there into the world and even make yourself vulnerable. Some of these exercises will be fun, others will scare and challenge you - but they are all designed to open your heart to more effective communication with others, so that the relationships you build are strong, heart centered and compassionate.

This book is written for anyone who feels that they are not living (and loving!) to their full potential. Whether you crave deeper connections with others or want to reignite relationships you are already in, this book was written to help you master the art of good communication.

In fact, it would be ideal for you to think of this book itself as one of the first of many new and interesting conversations you're going to have. Although I don't know you and cannot be sure of your response to what's written in these pages, I want for to engage with and respond to everything here as though I was sitting right there in the room with you.

You don't have to agree with everything, or like the principles outlined here. The important thing, though, is that in opening up the dialogue, you are already taking those first few steps to becoming more conscious, compassionate lovers and partners.

When we risk nothing, we gain nothing. When we don't open ourselves to love, we don't love deeply. My wish is that this book leaves you feeling open and receptive to love - your own ability to give it as well as the privilege of receiving it. And I hope that you have high expectations for yourself in reading it, too.

When two people come together, in any capacity, there is the chance for something special to happen. Every great romance began with a meeting of two hearts, with the first word of the first conversation. Let's begin this book with the first word. I am pleased to meet you, dear reader, and hope that in moving through this book together, we can jointly create a little more love, a little more tenderness and a little more understanding in the world than there was to begin with.

Download this book and continue reading by clicking <u>here</u>, or visit http://www.amazon.com/Simeon-Lindstrom/e/B00LHUJSAK/

Codependency - "Loves Me, Loves Me Not": Learn How To Cultivate Healthy Relationships, Overcome Relationship Jealousy, Stop Controlling Others and Be Codependent No More

If you've had difficulty with starting or maintaining relationships, issues with feeling jealous and possessive or find that your connections with others are more a source of distress than anything else, this book is for you.

By finding ways to be more mindful throughout the day, as well as exercises in improving your communication skills, this book will show you how to have relationships that are calmer and more stable and compassionate.

We'll begin with a look at the phenomenon of codependency, what it has traditionally meant in the psychological realm and how these traits and patterns can be traced back to issues of self-worth, compassion and more deliberate action. We'll examine how mindfulness can be the magic ingredient to getting a hold of the codependency cycle, and some of the characteristics of happy, mindful relationships. Finally, we'll explore a model for mindful communication and ways that you can begin to implement immediately in order to make a commitment to stronger, more compassionate relationships with others.

It may feel sometimes that an intense and serious connection with someone is proof of the depth of the feeling you have for one another. But be careful, obsession and dependency is not the same as love. In the codependent relationship, our affection and attention is coming from a place of fear and need. As a result, the partners never really connect with each other. They do endless, complicated dances around each others problems, but what they never do is make an honest human connection.

In codependent relationships, manipulation, guilt and resentment take the place of healthy, balanced affection. Codependent partners are not necessarily together because they want to be, they are because they have to be, because they don't know how to live otherwise. One partner may bring a history of abuse, a "personality disorder" or mental illness into a relationship; the ways the other partner responds to this may be healthy or not, but if they bring their own issues to the table too, they may find that the bond of their love is more accurately described as a shared and complementary dysfunction.

Remember, the relationships we are in can never be better than the relationships we have with ourselves. Two unhappy people together never make a happy couple together. We cannot treat other people in ways we have never taken the time to consider before, and we cannot communicate properly if we are not even sure what it is we need to communicate in the first place.

An individual with a mature, well-developed sense of themselves has the most to offer someone else. They have their own lives, their own sense of self-worth, their own strength. And when you remove need, fear, obsession and desperation, you open up the way for love and affection just for its own sake.

Love is many things, but it's cheapened when held hostage by the ego. Connections formed around ego and fear may be strong and lasting, but what keeps them going is mutual need. What could be more romantic than, "I don't need to be with you. You don't complete me at all. I am happy and stable and fulfilled without you. But I still want to be with you, because you're awesome"?

On the ground, in the nitty gritty of life, we can reduce a massive thing like "Relationships" down to smaller, more manageable units. Everything from the deepest and most profound romantic and spiritual union to sharing a joke with the cashier at the supermarket rests on one thing: communication. Whether it's through words or not, we are constantly communicating, and the accumulation of these little units creates this big thing we call a relationship.

Download this book and continue reading by clicking <u>here</u>, or visit http://www.amazon.com/Simeon-Lindstrom/e/B00LHUJSAK/

Mindful Eating: A Healthy, Balanced and Compassionate Way To Stop Overeating, How To Lose Weight and Get a Real Taste of Life by Eating Mindfully

What are you hungry for?

You may have been drawn to the idea of mindful eating as an antidote to the empty promises of the diet industry, or you may have felt that it's time to pursue a more purposeful, more compassionate way of eating. Whatever your reasons and whatever your current relationship to food and your body is, this book can help you reconsider your eating habits and whether they are truly serving your highest good.

Through an exploration of the real reasons we overeat, our thoughts and feelings around food, and coming into closer contact with our own true appetites, this book aims to help you craft an open and accepting attitude towards food.

Mindful eating is an attitude towards food (and much more) that encourages awareness, deliberate action and an open acceptance of the present moment as it unfolds around us.

In this book, we'll look at how the conventional dieting mindset is actually damaging and counterproductive, and how mindful eating can be a refreshing break away from all the expectations that you have about yourself and food that are not serving you. The ultimate goal is to become exquisitely tuned in to your own appetites, desires and passions, and to tune out the noise and clutter from the outside world that muffle your innate intuition about what is good for you and what isn't.

When we understand our true hunger, when we realize the psychological, emotional, behavioral, physical and even spiritual causes behind our overeating, only then can we can start to take realistic steps to remedy it.

Download this book and continue reading by clicking here, or visit http://www.amazon.com/Simeon-Lindstrom/e/B00LHUJSAK/

Minimalism: How To Declutter, De-Stress And Simplify Your Life With Simple Living

Today, a growing number of people are becoming dissatisfied with their lives and turning to simpler ways of working, living and raising their children.

This book will explore the philosophy of minimalism and how it can streamline your life, declutter your home, reduce stress, mindless consumerism, and reconnect you to what's truly important.

You'll find ways to adopt a mindset that promotes simplicity and elegance in your every day life, and rethink your dependence on material possessions. We will explore how practical changes to our surroundings can lead to a previously unknown inner peace and calm. Whether in our wardrobes, kitchens, work lives or our deeper sense of personal and spiritual purpose, we could all do with focusing on things that align with our values and reducing the distraction of those things that pull us away from them. This book shows you how.

For those born and raised in the height of our consumer society, the idea that happiness and personal fulfillment is found in stuff is more or less a given. The capitalist machine we all live within requires only one thing of us: that we should constantly want, and the things we should want are to be found, usually, in malls. Malls that are filled with strategically placed advertising, with the sole purpose to entice and lure you, trying to convince you that you need, not want, their specific product. Our economy relies heavily on a steady stream of consumption: better clothes, cars, bigger houses and things to fill those houses with, the newest appliances, Christmas decorations, pet toys, jewelry, office furniture, pot plants, gaming consoles, specialty tires, luxury soaps... the array of stuff is simply dazzling.

But if you are reading this there's a chance you find this overabundance just a little... exhausting. Paradoxically, there seems to be a sad sort of emptiness in filling up one's life with more things. What is simple and truly valuable often seems to be completely hidden under mountains of what is unnecessary. Although advertising tells us the best way to solve problems is to buy solutions, tranquility and a graceful life seem to elude us, no matter what we buy or how much of it.

Minimalism is an aesthetic, a philosophy and a way of life. This book takes a look at how deeply liberating a simpler life can be, and shows you ways you can adopt a calmer, more deliberate way of living and working. Minimalism is about clearing away the clutter that is distracting from what is really important. It's about rethinking our attitudes to ownership, to our lifestyles and to our innermost values.

Download this book and continue reading by clicking here, or visit http://www.amazon.com/Simeon-Lindstrom/e/B00LHUJSAK/

Self-Esteem For Kids - Every Parent's Greatest Gift: How To Raise Kids To Have Confidence In Themselves And Their Own Abilities

This book will help you learn how self-esteem develops in children. It will also give you step-by-step instructions for building up your child's self-esteem in a natural way. The ultimate goal of this book is to help you build and maintain your child's self-esteem, as well as help raise their self-esteem if it has fallen to an all-time low.

Many parents do not recognize the importance of self-esteem. Even if they know that it is important, they are not aware of how self-esteem develops or what they can do to help. However, the fact of the matter is that parents are the primary influence on a child's self-esteem. High self-esteem and self-confidence are the greatest gifts you can give your child.

With high self-esteem, your child will be able to succeed in school and in life. They will have healthy relationships, become successful in their chosen career, and be able to live productive and happy lives. Self-esteem is a necessary tool for them to have as they grow and become adults. By giving them this gift you will be giving them the most precious gift of all—happiness.

Great self-esteem is one of the most important gifts you will ever give your child. But what is it exactly? How do you define something so seemingly elusive? Self-esteem simply defined is having confidence in one's self, worth and abilities. It is about self-respect. A child cannot develop self-esteem if they feel that they are worthless in any way. Likewise they cannot build self-esteem if they feel that there is nothing they are good at, or that they have no talents.

Self-esteem, in the end, is all about self-worth. What does your child think they are worth? Do they recognize how much they mean to you, and how important they are to you and the world around them? Do they understand that everyone has set backs, but everyone also has talents and abilities that increase their worth? Does your child know what these abilities and talents are?

Most of these questions would be hard to answer. It is difficult to ask these types of questions to young children. They often do not understand what you want them to say. In older children the questions are just as useless because the child will likely lie or simply refuse to answer. As a parent it is your job to judge your child's self-esteem based on actions, moods and temperaments.

Please keep in mind while reading this book that while every child is different, all children need these things in their lives. You know your child best, but at least most of the strategies and tips in this book will apply.

Download this book and continue reading by clicking here, or visit http://www.amazon.com/Simeon-Lindstrom/e/BooLHUJSAK/

Made in the USA
Middletown, DE
07 September 2016